양성수 디카시집
Dica (Digital Camera) Poems
by Yang Seong-soo

디카詩, 삶에 장착하다

Life Equipped with Dica Poems

번역 • 우형숙
translated by Woo Hyeong-sook

창연

디카詩,
삶에 장착하다

Life Equipped with Dica Poems

작가의 말

정답도 오답도 없는 세상에서
내 인생의 스승은 삶에서 부서져 나온 파편들이었습니다.
그 파편들을 모아 한 권의 책으로 엮었습니다.

바쁘신 시간에도 교열을 봐주신 문학평론가 민충환 교수님,
초대작가로 참여해주신 구자룡 원로 시인님,
또한 번역해주신 우형숙 교수님께 감사 말씀드립니다.

2021년 8월

유네스코문학 창의도시
부천에서

‖ preface ‖

In this world where there's no right or wrong answer, I've learned a lot from ups and downs in life.
This book weaves together the various strands of my life.

I extend my heartfelt gratitude to Prof. Min Chung-hwan, who was busy, but willingly proofread all my poems.
I'm deeply indebted to the poet Koo Ja-ryong, who joined in this book as an invited poet.
Also I'm grateful to Prof. Woo Hyeong-sook, who translated my poems into English.

August, 2021

UNESCO Creative City of Literature
Bucheon, Korea

차례

작가의 말 ‖ preface ‖   004

디카詩, 삶에 장착하다
Life Equipped with Dica Poems

시詩 Poem 013
행복 창고 Storage for Happiness 015
세상에서 가장 아름다운 이야기
The Most Beautiful Word in the World 017
세상사 How to Live in the World 019
멍에 Yoke 021
무소유욕 Spirit of Nonpossession 023
버스 타고 그랜드 캐니언에 가다
Going to the Grand Canyon by Bus 025
도道 Route 027
보트피플 Boat People 029
다비식 Cremation Rite 031
창 Window 033
기억하라 Remember 035
나를 찾아서 In Search of Myself 037
삶을 대하는 방법 How to Cope with Life 039
타임캡슐 Time Capsule 041

데칼코마니 Decalcomanie 043
원미산의 봄 Spring of Mt. Wonmi 045
가을 명세서 The Specification in Autumn 047
등 맞대고 가야 할 길
The Way to Go with Our Backs to Each Other 049
나는 지금 무엇을 심고 있나 What Am I Planting Now? 051
여정 Journey 053
우리 가야 할 길 The Way We Should Go 055
사랑 Love 057
그러더이다 Yes, Indeed 059
마음의 문 The Door of Your Mind 061
가을, 나에게 묻다 Autumn Asks Me 063
푸르른 삶 Green Life 065
인생 방정식 Life Equation 067
암각화 Rock Art 069
블루카펫 Blue Carpet 071

관계론 Relationship Theory 073
빛과 그림자 Light and Shadow 075
만들어 가는 인생 The Life We Make 077
나, 그리고 너 I And You 079
살만한 세상 A World Worth Living In 081
두려움 떨쳐내고 Shaking Off Fear 083
산에서 듣다 I Hear This at the Mountain 085
족하다 It's Enough 087
아프냐 Are You Sick? 089
다름의 미학 Aesthetics of Difference 091
버킷리스트 Bucket List 093
두려움 Fear 095
그림 그리기 Drawing 097
얼룩 Stain 099

울지 마라 Don't Cry 101
알고 보면 On Further Acquaintance 103
'아'와 '어' 사이 Between 'Ah' and 'Uh' 105
고향, 그해 겨울 Hometown, That Winter 107
차마 I Just Can't 109
마음 얻는 길 A Way to Win the Heart 111
실패해 보지 않은 삶 Living Without Failing 113
사실은 In Fact 115
그래, 그래 Yes Yes 117
서러운 5월에 In the Sad Month of May 119
바람의 흉터 Scar of the Wind 121
부모 Parents 123
언제나 하나였다 Always One 125
무대 위 주인공은 너야 The Hero of the Stage Is You 127
살아내기 Survival 129

‖ **초대 디카시: 구자룡** 시인
　Invitation: Dica Poem by Koo Ja-ryong 130

‖ **양성수** 시인 소개
　About the Poet Yang Seong-soo 132
‖ 번역자 **우형숙** 소개
　About the Translator Woo Hyeong-sook 134

디카詩, 삶에 장착하다
Life Equipped with Dica Poems

＊ The subject in the photo looks just like the Korean word 'ㅅㅣ'(poem).

시 詩

마음밭 쭉정이 걸러내고
알곡들 추수하여 식탁에 올려지는 음식이다

Poem

A poem is food that's put on a table,
as we separate chaff from grain to make food.

행복 창고

너!

Storage for Happiness

It's you!

세상에서 가장 아름다운 이야기

용서

The Most Beautiful Word in the World

Forgiveness

세상사

응달 마음 거두면 지천이 봄이다

How to Live in the World

If we get sadness of our heart, it's spring every-where.

멍에

한 굽이 지나가면 스르륵 녹아내리고야 말

Yoke

If we pass the curve of the street, the yokes fade away, like melting snow.

무소유욕

울타리에도 걸리지 않는 바람처럼

Spirit of Nonpossession

It's like the wind that doesn't get caught even by the fence.

버스 타고 그랜드 캐니언에 가다

마음이 길이다

Going to the Grand Canyon by Bus

Your mind is the way.

도道

눈에 보이지 않는다
하여 뱃길이 없는 것은 아니었다

Route

It is invisible to the eyes.
But we are not without a sea route.

보트피플

Help me!
Help me!

Boat People

Help me!
Help me!

다비식

불,
살랐다.

Cremation Rite

I set it
on fire.

창

마음의 문
여는 만큼 보이려니

Window

The window of the heart;
the more we open up, the more we will see.

기억하라

오늘의 이 찬란한 아침은
어제의 비바람과 함께 온 선물이려니

Remember

This brilliant morning is a gift
that came with rainstorm yesterday.

나를 찾아서

봄은 봄이라 말하고
산은 산이라 말하네

In Search of Myself

Spring says, "I am spring";
A mountain says, "I am a mountain."

삶을 대하는 방법

그림자 없는 인생길이 어디 있으랴
떼려야 뗄 수 없다면 태양을 마주 향해 가라

How to Cope with Life

Where is a life with no shadows?
If you cannot remove your shadow, walk toward the sun.

타임캡슐

오뉘,
어느 봄날.

Time Capsule

Sweet brother and sister,
one spring day

데칼코마니

파도는 파도를 만들지만
주름은 인성을 만든다

Decalcomanie

Waves make waves;
wrinkles make personality.

원미산의 봄

춘풍春風 도령!
자네, 밥은 먹고 다니시는가?

Spring of Mt. Wonmi

Gentle spring breeze!
Did you have meals?

가을 명세서

넌, 한 해를 잘 살아내어 곱게 물들고
난, 한평생 곱게만 살아오지 못해 얼굴 붉히고

The Specification in Autumn

You've lived well for a year, so you are beautiful now.
But I haven't lived well all my life, so I'm red-faced.

등 맞대고 가야 할 길

우리네
결코 홀로 갈 수 없다는 사실을 내 아노니

The Way to Go with Our Backs to Each Other

As I know,
we can never go alone.

나는 지금 무엇을 심고 있나

밑동 잘린 그루터기도
구름꽃 피워내거늘

What Am I Planting Now?

Even a tree stump
put out some flowers that look like clouds.

여정

함께인 듯 싶어도 홀로 가야 할 길
홀로인 듯 싶어도 함께 가야 할 길

Journey

Though we seem to go together, we go alone.
Though we seem to go alone, we go together.

우리 가야 할 길

꽃은 시들지라도
그 향기의 기억은 시들지 않는다

The Way We Should Go

Though flowers wither,
the memories of the scents don't fade.

사랑

눈높이 마주하지 않고
온전한 맘 전해질 수 없느니

Love

If you don't get down to their level,
you can't show your true mind.

그러더이다

살아보니 견뎌지더이다
견뎌보니 살아지더이다

Yes, Indeed

Living a life, I could endure hardships.
Enduring life, I could survive.

마음의 문

열어젖히면 빛의 세상이요
달아걸면 어둠의 세계라

The Door of Your Mind

If you open the door, you'll be in the world of light.
If you close the door, you'll be in a world of darkness.

가을, 나에게 묻다

너는 지금 아름답게 물들고 있느냐
낙엽 되어 떨어진들 여한 없는 삶이었더냐

Autumn Asks Me

Are you turning into beautiful colors now?
You're a fallen leaf; did you live without regrets?

푸르른 삶

저마다 가슴에
울타리는 세우되
울에 얽매이지는 말자

Green Life

Though we each make a fence
in our minds,
let's not be tied up there.

인생 방정식

1+1=1
1+1=2
1+1=3

Life Equation

1+1=1
1+1=2
1+1=3

암각화

모래와 파도는
바윗덩어리와 부대끼면서도
아름다운 세월을 그려낸다

Rock Art

Sand and waves,
troubled with rocks,
draw beautiful times.

블루카펫

우리 가는 길
돌덩이처럼 차디찬 세상일지라도
길목마다 아름다운 날들도 준비되어 있다

Blue Carpet

Though we're going
in the world that is as cold as a rock,
we'll have beautiful days at every street corner.

관계론

생살이라도 도려내어
내 것을 내주어야
네가 들어올 수 있음이여

Relationship Theory

When my flesh is dug out
and given away,
O you can come into me.

빛과 그림자

세상은 빛과 어둠의 세계라

빛이 있는 곳에 그림자 생겨나니
그 뒤에는 빛이 있음이라

Light and Shadow

It's the world of light and darkness.

Where there is light, shadows are formed.
Behind them, there is light.

만들어 가는 인생

눈앞
네모난 세상 아무것 보이지 않는 듯해도
렌즈의 초점 마주 닿는 곳마다 새로운 세상이 펼쳐진다

The Life We Make

In front of you, there's a square-shaped world.
It seems there's nothing visible.
But focus the camera on anything, and you will see a new world.

나, 그리고 너

태양이 솟아오르면
하늘도 벌겋게 물드는데
나는 누구에게 어떤 빛으로 기억될까

I And You

When the sun rises
the sky turns red.
How will I be remembered to somebody?

살만한 세상

등나무 줄기처럼
세상살이 얽히고 설킨듯 해도
온 천지 아우르는 한 점 빛 있거늘

A World Worth Living In

Just like wistaria vines,
everything in the world seems to get entangled.
But there's a light encompassing the whole world.

두려움 떨쳐내고

가보지 않은 길이라
지레 포기하지 마소

가보지 않은 길은 있을지라도
갈 수 없는 길은 없음이니

Shaking Off Fear

Though a road wasn't taken before,
don't give up the road beforehand.

Though there's a road that wasn't taken,
there's no road that we can't take.

산에서 듣다

굳이
마음 닦거나 씻어내려 하지 마소
해가 가면 닦여지고
비 오면 씻겨지리니

I Hear This at the Mountain

Don't try
to polish or wash the mind.
As time goes by, it'll be polished.
When it rains, it'll be washed.

족하다

쪽빛 바다가 아니면 어떠랴

갯골 드러난 물빛 흐리다
하지만
아름다움이 어찌 물빛 뿐이랴

It's Enough

What though the sea isn't clear blue?

The water, on the tidal flat, looks murky.
But how can we say
its beauty depends only on the color?

아프냐

마음 퍼렇게 멍든 사람아
하늘을 보라

너도 저처럼 맑은 하늘 닮으려
그렇게 아프나 보다

Are You Sick?

Oh Man who is sick at heart,
look up at the sky.

I daresay you are so sick,
as you want to resemble the clear sky.

다름의 미학

그 푸르던 녹색이 형형색색 단풍으로
단풍은 다시 낙엽으로 흔적 없이 사라졌지만
한결같은 외고집
너 홀로 겨울을 지키고 있구나

Aesthetics of Difference

The green leaves turned into colorful leaves,
and the autumn leaves fell and disappeared.
However, you are single-minded,
upholding winter all by yourself.

버킷리스트

피로와 함께 마시는 커피 한 모금

저녁 식사 후,
아삭한 사과 한 개

TV 보며 느긋하게 마시는 숭늉 한 사발

Bucket List

Taking a gulp of coffee to recover from fatigue.

Munching an apple
after dinner.

Enjoying a bowl of scorched-rice water, with TV on.

두려움

파도 없는 바다 어디 있을까
오대양 어느 곳일지라도

그래,
출렁이는 흔들림은 배 띄우기 위함인 걸

Fear

Among the Five Oceans,
which ocean doesn't have waves?

Yes,
to set a ship afloat, the waves roll and crash.

그림 그리기

누구는
녹슨 세월 위에 봉황 둥지도 트는데

내
이 청명 하늘에 무슨 꿈인들 못 그릴까

Drawing

Someone
built a nest for a phoenix on the rusty iron pole.

I daresay
I can draw any dreams in the clear blue sky.

얼룩

살다보면 김칫국물 튀길 수도 있지만

이겨도 지는 다툼 이기려 하지 말고
이길 수 없는 다툼 이기려 하지 말며
이겨도 되는 다툼 져준들 어떻겠소

Stain

While living, you may spatter Kimchi liquid.

Don't try to win the fight that makes all losers;
don't try to win the fight that you can never win;
lose the fight that you may win, won't you?

울지 마라

한 번쯤 인생에 금이 간들 어떠랴

겨울 강가 얼음장 쩍
쩍 갈라지는 소리도 알고 보니
봄이 오는 소리였다

Don't Cry

What though you have a crack at least once while living?

When the ice cracked by the winter river,
the sound of the cracking
was that of the coming spring.

알고 보면

꽃인들 예쁜 날만 있었을까

줄기에 튀기던 흙물
꽃잎 흔들던 바람소리
꽃봉오리 적시던 찬이슬도 있었음에

On Further Acquaintance

Though they're flowers, do they have only pretty days?

Muddy water splashes on the stems;
the wind hits the petals;
cold dews wet the flower buds.

'아'와 '어' 사이

빈 깡통이 요란하다며
발로
콱 밟아 버린 이여

누군가의 눈에는 모두가 보석이었다

Between 'Ah' and 'Uh'

Grumbling that empty cans creak most,
someone crushed the cans
with his feet.

But all the cans were gems to someone else.

고향, 그해 겨울

살았고

있었고
그랬고

문풍지 휘파람 소리에
호롱불 춤추었고

Hometown, That Winter

Someone lived there.

Something was there.
Yes, it was.

With the whistling of paper weather strips,
the flame of a kerosene lamp danced.

차마

이제껏
떨구었던 말들
보여주었던 민낯 들고서
이 고운 꽃들을 어찌 밟으랴

I Just Can't

Up to now
lots of words have come out of my mouth.
Without any makeup on,
how can I step on these pretty flowers?

마음 얻는 길

돌덩이로 쌓아 올렸던 아집의 성城
견고했던 성벽 한쪽 모서리 깨뜨려가며
네가 들어올 수 있는 작은 길 만들었을 때
새로운 관계가 그곳으로부터 시작됨을 알겠노니

A Way to Win the Heart

A stone castle of sheer obstinacy.
Demolishing an edge of the substantial rampart,
I made a path so that you could enter it.
From it, our new relationship started.

실패해 보지 않은 삶

실
패
한

인생이다

Living Without Failing

Such
a
life

is a failure.

사실은

하늘이 제 높다 해도
누구든 바라볼 수 있다

하늘이 제 넓다 해도
요만큼이면 족하다

못할 것도 더할 것도 없다

In Fact

No matter how high the sky is,
anybody can see it.

No matter large the sky is,
this size is enough to me.

No more and no less.

그래, 그래

누군들 금수저길 곁눈질하지 않았을까마는
삶이 가야 했던 길은 굽이진 길

문득
옛길 파노라마 펼쳐지니
굽이 굽이졌던 길이어서 더 아름다웠던 길

Yes Yes

Who wouldn't cast glances upon a golden road;
But I had to go on a crooked path.

Casually
I see the nostalgia lane in a panorama;
the old path was prettier, as it was winding.

서러운 5월에

등
따끈한 햇살 앞에
내 안에 박힌 가시 하나 뽑아내고

그 자리
오월 한 그루 심는다

In the Sad Month of May

In the sunshine
that warms up my back,
I pull out a thorn from me.

Into the place
I put the month May.

바람의 흉터

때로는
세상에 긁히고 날카로움에 베이지만

나뭇가지 붙잡고 울지언정
그 생채기
흉터로 남기지는 않는다

Scar of the Wind

Sometimes
trees are scraped or cut by the world.

Taking boughs or twigs, the wind may weep.
But the scratches
don't become scars.

부모

바다를 그저 바다려니 하지 마라
바닷빛은 언제나 초록빛이려니 하지 마라

바다도 마음이 갈래 지어 퍼렇게 멍들 때가 있다
바다도 때로는 마음이 산산이 부서지는 날이 있다
바다도 그런 날에는 갈매기 울음을 토한다

Parents

Don't say that a sea is just a sea.
Don't say that the color of the sea is always blue.

Even the sea is sometimes broken-hearted.
Even the sea is sometimes smashed to pieces.
On such days, the sea cries as if seagulls cry.

언제나 하나였다

하늘
그리고 땅과 바다
어디엔들 38선이 그어져 있으랴

시퍼런 서해 바다, 남과 북 한데 섞이는
아, 백령도여!

Always One

The sky,
the land and the sea.
The 38th parallel is nowhere to be seen.

South and North blend together in the West Sea.
Oh Baengnyeong Island!

무대 위 주인공은 너야

움츠리거나
두려워할 이유는 없다

바람이 불어오는 방향 향해
고개 쳐들고
발가락에 힘주고

The Hero of the Stage Is You

You don't need to crouch down or feel scared.

Raise your head
to windward,
and clench your toes.

살아내기

요동치는 땅거죽 위 멀미하는 이여!

몸은 비틀거릴지라도
마음만은 비틀거리지 말자

마음은 비틀거릴지라도
몸만은 비틀거리지 말자

우리.

Survival

O man, who feels dizzy on the rolling land!

Though our bodies stagger,
let's not make our minds stagger.

Though our minds stagger,
let's not make our bodies stagger.

You and I.

‖ 초대 디카시: 구자룡 시인 작품 ‖

* 지하철역 화장실 디카시 전시에서

* At the Dica Poetry Exhibition of the Subway Station Restroom

‖ Invitation: Dica Poem by Koo Ja-ryong ‖

喜 · 喜

와
오줌이 잘 나와

Joy · Joy

Wow
Urine comes out well.

구자룡: 시인 · 한국작가회의 회원 · 부천작가회의 고문
저서 60여권

Koo Ja-ryong: poet · member of the Writers' Association of Korea · adviser of the Bucheon Writers' Association. He has published over 60 books.

‖ **양성수** 시인 소개 ‖

시인, 디카詩 문학평론가
한국 작가회의 부천지부 회원

부천 디카시협회 회원

『자네, 밥은 먹고 다니시는가』 외 시집 3권
개인 디카시 시화전 8회
건국경제신문 창세예술대상 수상
부천시민신문 디카詩 연재 중(2018~   )
일간경기신문 디카詩 연재 중(2021~   )

‖ About the Poet **Yang Seong-soo** ‖

   As a poet and dica poem critic, he is a member of the Writers' Association of Korea-Bucheon Branch and also a member of the Bucheon Dica Poets' Association.

   He published three poetry books, including *Did You Have a Meal?* He held eight solo Dica poetry exhibitions. He received the *Changse* Arts Award from the Geonkuk Business Newspaper. He's been writing Dica poems for the Bucheon Citizens' Newspaper since 2018. He's been writing Dica poems for the Daily Kyunggi Newspaper since 2021.

‖ 번역자 **우형숙** 소개 ‖

시조시인. 번역가. 現 국제 PEN 한국본부 번역위원장. 국제계관시인연합회 번역위원. 한국현대시인협회 번역위원. 한국문인협회 시조분과 번역팀장. 부천작가회의회장 역임. 영문학박사(시 번역 전공). 모교인 숙명여자대학교(25년)와 세종대학교(5년)에서 영문학 및 번역 강의(겸임교수). 2017년 은퇴 후, 지금까지 시집 및 시조집 10여 권을 번역함.

About the Translator **Woo Hyeong-sook**

As a sijo poetess and translator, she serves as the head of the translation committee at the International PEN-Korean Centre. She is a translation committee member for the United Poets Laureate International as well as the Modern Korean Poets' Association. She is also a leading translator for the sijo division of the Korean Writers' Association. She was the president of the Bucheon Writers' Association. She holds a doctorate in English literature (major: poetry translation). She taught English literature and translation at her alma mater, Sookmyung Women's University for 25 years and Sejong University for 5 years as an adjunct professor. She has translated over 10 collections of poetry and sijo poetry into English since she retired in 2017.

창연디카시선 008

디카詩, 삶에 장착하다

2021년 9월 18일 발행

지 은 이 | 양성수
편 집 인 | 이소정
펴 낸 이 | 임창연
펴 낸 곳 | 창연출판사
주   소 | 경남 창원시 의창구 읍성로 39
출판등록 | 2013년 11월 26일 제2013-000029호
전   화 | (055) 296-2030
팩   스 | (055) 246-2030
E - mail | 7calltaxi@hanmail.net

값 20,000원
ISBN 979-11-91751-05-5   03810

ⓒ 양성수, 2021

* 이 책의 판권은 저자와 창연출판사에 있습니다.
* 양측의 서면 동의 없이 무단 전재나 복제를 금합니다.